NATIONAL
GEOGRAPHIC

Communities Around th

Coober Pedy
Australia

Elspeth Leacock

PICTURE CREDITS
Cover, page 24 (left) Richard I'Anson/Lonely Planet Images; Cover (inset) Ted Spiegel/Corbis; pages 1 (left), 14, 15 (bottom) South Australian Tourism Commission; pages 1 (right), 8 (top left) Jordi Vidal-V&W/Bruce Coleman Inc.; page 2 (top) Christopher Groenhout/Lonely Planet Images; page 2 (bottom) Alfred Pasieka/Science Photo Library/Photo Researchers; pages 3, 4, 8–9 (bottom), 12, 20 (top), 20–21 (right) Paul A. Souders/Corbis; pages 5, 22 (bottom) Bill Bachman; pages 6 (top), 15 (top) Getty Images; page 6 (bottom) Carl and Ann Purcell/Corbis; pages 8 (top right), 10 (top, middle, bottom), 24 (right) Carl Purcell; p. 9 (top) Derek Halstead/Getty Images; page 9 (right) Patrick Ward/Corbis; page 10–11 Diana Mayfield/Lonely Planet Images; page 11 Charles & Josette Lenars/Corbis; pages 12-13, 18 (middle), 18-19 (bottom) AFP/CORBIS; pages 16 (top), 16–17 (bottom), 22 (top) Courtesy/Stephen Staines; page 17 (right) The Kobal Collection; pages 18 (top), 20 (bottom) Ross Barnett/Lonely Planet Images; page 19 (right) Adam Bruzzone; page 23 Adams/Hansen Photography.

Maps:
Dave Stevenson

Produced through the worldwide resources of the National Geographic Society, John M. Fahey, Jr., President and Chief Executive Officer; Gilbert M. Grosvenor, Chairman of the Board; Nina D. Hoffman, Executive Vice President and President, Books and School Publishing.

PREPARED BY NATIONAL GEOGRAPHIC SCHOOL PUBLISHING
Ericka Markman, Senior Vice President; Steve Mico, Vice President, Editorial Director; Marianne Hiland, Editorial Manager; Jim Hiscott, Design Manager; Kristin Hanneman, Illustrations Manager; Matt Wascavage, Manager of Publishing Services; Sean Philpotts, Production Manager.

Production: Clifton M. Brown III, Manufacturing and Quality Control

PROGRAM DEVELOPMENT
Gare Thompson Associates, Inc.

BOOK DEVELOPMENT
Thomas Nieman, Inc.

CONSULTANTS/REVIEWERS
Dr. Margit E. McGuire, School of Education, Seattle University, Seattle, Washington
Stephen Staines, Tourist Information Officer
District Council of Coober Pedy

BOOK DESIGN
Steven Curtis Design, Inc.

Published by the National Geographic Society
1145 17th Street, N.W.
Washington, D.C. 20036–4688

ISBN: 0-7922-8618-9

Fourth Printing July 2004
Printed in Canada

Coober

Table of Contents

Miner going underground to hunt for opals

Welcome to Coober Pedy,

a community in Australia. Hi! Or, as we say here, "G'day!" My hometown doesn't look like much. But there's a lot more to see here than first meets the eye. That's because a lot of people here live and work underground!

First, I'll show you where Coober Pedy (KOO–ber PEE–dee) is. Then you will see why this small town grew up in the middle of nowhere. We'll go underground where miners can strike it rich or come up empty-handed.

Next, we'll visit my home, and you can see what it's like to live underground. We'll also spend a day at my school.

Last, I'll show you around town. You'll see how people here live and what we do for fun. You'll see where we worship and how we govern ourselves. You'll meet a lot of new people in Coober Pedy. Be sure to wish them "G'day."

My name is Darcy. I live here in Coober Pedy. Come along, and I'll show you around.

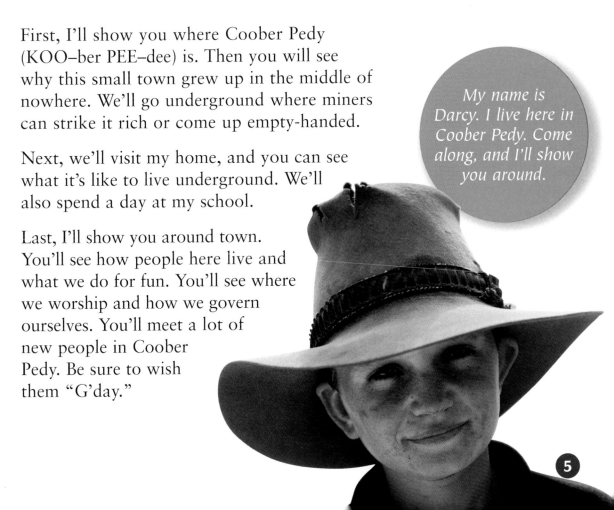

5

CHAPTER 1

A Town in the Outback

Tough Climate

To find Coober Pedy, you have to find Australia first. That's pretty easy because Australia is the only country in the world that is a whole **continent**. You know what continents are, right? They are the biggest bodies of land on earth.

First, find the **equator** on the globe. It is an imaginary line that divides the earth into two parts. Australia is in the southern half, below the equator. That is why it's called the land "down under."

The middle of Australia is a huge dry plain called the **outback**. The **climate** is too hot and dry for just about anything to grow. Coober Pedy is in the outback. But don't worry. I'll show you how we stay cool and comfortable here.

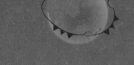

INDIAN
OCEAN

Coral Sea

Australia

Coober Pedy •

★ Canberra

MILES
0   250   500   750

0   750
KILOMETERS

Equator

AUSTRALIA

You must wonder why anybody would want to live in a place like this. Coober Pedy's story began when a 15-year-old boy named Willie Hutchinson went exploring. He came here in 1915 with his dad to look for gold. Willie finished his chores at their camp and started to look around. He didn't find any gold, but he did find beautiful, milky-colored stones with sparks of green and pink. They were **opals**. Willie had discovered the richest opal field in the world.

A large opal can be worth $10,000 or more! So people began to come here hoping to find their fortunes. Let's go to an opal mine.

Street scene in Coober Pedy

It's nice and cool down here. People used to work mines with picks and shovels. Today, miners use explosives, and big machines do most of the digging. Then the miners search through the loosened rock and dirt for opals. When they are done, the leftover dirt is dumped in huge piles.

Let's search a pile. We call that **"noodling."** People often find opals that the miners missed. But be careful! Don't fall down a mine hole. These mine holes can be very deep.

Strine

Ever heard of "strine"? That's what we call Australian slang. You know two words in strine already—"G'day" and "noodling." Here are a few more:

bludger lazy

dag nerd

dinkum real, genuine

go walkabout wander around

grouse excellent, wonderful, terrific

mate friend, pal

wowser someone who likes to spoil the fun

What are these tourists doing? That's right, noodling for opals.

A View from Above

Let's go up. You get a very special view of Coober Pedy from an airplane. Up here, you can see for miles. And as far as you can see, the ground is covered with bumps. There are hundreds and hundreds of them. Do you remember when we went noodling in a pile of dirt? Well, all of those mounds are piles of dirt left behind by miners.

From up here, the mine holes and dirt piles look about the same. But down below, things are different. In some mines, people got rich. In others, they worked for months and found nothing.

Coober Pedy's miners are not all the same either. They come from about 45 different countries. There are miners from faraway places like Greece and Italy. Others are Australians who moved here from the cities.

There are **Aborigines** too. They are the first Australians, like Native Americans are the first Americans. They came here thousands of years before anyone else. My town's name comes from their language. "Kupa piti" means "white man down a hole." Can you guess why the town got that name?

Faces you might see in a mine in Coober Pedy

From above, the area around Coober Pedy looks like ant hills.

Earth's Voice

Like Native Americans, Aborigines are not one group but many groups. Each group has its own music and dance and art. But Aborigines also share some things. Have you ever heard the sound of a **didgeridoo**? It is a big flute with a very deep tone. Musicians from many different Aborigine groups play it. Some people say that, if the earth had a voice, it would sound like a didgeridoo.

Aborigine playing a didgeridoo

11

CHAPTER 2

At Home and School

Living Underground

In Coober Pedy, most of our homes are underground. We call them "dugouts." Today you are invited to visit my home and meet my family. It is nice and cool inside. Outside, the temperature can be cold on a winter night or very hot on a summer day. But inside it always stays comfortable. Remember, that's without heaters or air conditioners.

Our home is big. We have a kitchen, a bathroom, and a big living room. Many of these rooms have windows. We each have our own bedroom! Some people have their own underground swimming pool!

When my friend had a new baby sister, his family just dug a new room. Since this is Coober Pedy, you never know what you will find when you dig. They found opals worth $3,000!

A family in their underground home

A quiet place underground for reading

A Cool Dugout!

How do we make a dugout? First, we use a bulldozer to cut away part of a natural hill. Then we use big machines called **boggers** to dig tunnels into the hillside. A bogger cuts the underground rooms quickly and easily.

People sometimes ask me what are the good and bad things about living underground. One very good thing is the thick walls. You can play your music as loud as you want!

What things aren't so great about living underground? There are no windows in our bedrooms, so when the light's out, it's pitch-black, like a cave. Otherwise, it's fine.

This is my brother. I like to hang out in his room sometimes.

Kitchen in an underground home

A Day at School

It is Cultural Awareness Week at school, and you are invited! My school is not a dugout. But you don't have to worry about the heat. The school is air-conditioned.

The students here can teach each other about many different cultures. We are cultural experts. Do you know why? Do you remember how people from faraway places came to mine opals? Well, those miners brought their families with them.

The students in my school are from countries in Europe like Greece, Italy, and Slovenia. There are Asians from Indonesia and the Philippines. And there are Australians and Aborigines too. The students here are from 35 different countries.

COOBER PEDY AREA SCHOOL
Welcomes you
ΕΛΣ ΚΑΛΟΣΟΡΙΖΟΜΕ • NGALYA-TJARPA.
ДОБРО ДОШЛИ • BENEVUTI.
DOBRO DOSLI • SZIVESEN LÁTTOT.

This sign says "welcome" in the languages of some of the places where my classmates come from.

16

Here's one of my friends

Whew! That's a lot of cultures. Imagine a week of sharing. We eat lots of good food. We sing songs in 20 languages. We share stories and pictures from around the world!

The subjects we study in school are a lot like yours. We also do a lot of camping and learn about the **environment** too. What I like most about my school is that it has its own radio station. It is called Dusty Radio. When I get older, I want to have my own radio show about sports. Some of our sports may seem strange to you. We play a ballgame called "cricket." But we also play softball, football, soccer, and indoor hockey.

Local Culture

A Trip to Mars?

There are some special visitors to Coober Pedy. They are film crews. Some people think the outback around Coober Pedy looks like another planet. The ground here is red—like on Mars. So when a crew was filming "Red Planet" in 1999, they came here. Want to feel like an astronaut? Come see us!

Actors exploring "Mars" in Coober Pedy

CHAPTER 3

Around Coober Pedy

Above and Below

Today we are going to explore Coober Pedy.
There are five churches in town, but you can't find them by looking for their steeples. Can you guess why? All the churches are underground! We can visit underground stores, restaurants—even a museum.

One of our underground churches

We can do things above ground too. A good place to get a look at Coober Pedy is from the Big Winch. (You can see it on the top of page 18.) It's in the shape of a really big hand winch. That's a machine miners used in the old days to bring dirt up from the mines.

Have you ever played golf? We have a golf course in Coober Pedy. But don't expect to play on green grass. Our golf course is grass-free!

Why is our golf course grassless? It's because water is too valuable to use for growing grass. Our water is pumped to Coober Pedy from a source a long distance away. People here have enough water, but we must be careful not to waste any. Each family and each business pays for the water it uses.

A "green" on our golf course

Tough Critters

What can live with little water, hot days, and cold nights? Lizards! There are lots of strange-looking lizards here. There are also snakes and spiders. A few large animals live here too. You might run into a **kangaroo**, a **camel**, or an **emu** in the outback. Kangaroos are native to Australia. Camels aren't. They were brought here to work in the dry outback. Emus are birds that are so big and heavy that they can't fly.

A kangaroo crossing sign

A Festival of Opals

Today, all the finest opals in town are on display.
It is the Coober Pedy Opal Festival. The whole town is crowded with people who want to go on the special opal walk. So grab a map to see where to go.

Our first stop is the Old Timers Mine. This was once a real working opal mine. It shows visitors how miners worked the old way—with picks and shovels. We'll look at opals at the underground opal store and museum. We could even buy an opal. But we have more places to go and more opals to see. If you finish the whole walk and are lucky, you can win a special prize. It is an opal worth $1,000!

Lots of tourists come to see our town and our opals. About 100,000 tourists visit every year. They like seeing life in a small mining town. They eat in our restaurants and stay in our hotels and motels. Tourism has helped Coober Pedy grow. Look at this sign for a local shop. It's a car painted to look like an opal!

Children at the festival

Index